JUSTICE

Under a system of true justice, everyone starts from the same place and has an equal opportunity to achieve what is rightfully due them.

JUSTICE

Kevin Osborn

THE ROSEN PUBLISHING GROUP, INC.
NEW YORK

Published in 1992 by The Rosen Publishing Group, Inc.
29 East 21st Street, New York, NY 10010.

First Edition
Copyright © 1992 by the Rosen Publishing Group, Inc.

Printed in Canada

Library of Congress Cataloging-in-Publication Data

Osborn, Kevin, 1951–
      Justice / Kevin Osborn.
      (The Values library)
      Includes bibliographical references and index.
      Summary: Discusses the meaning of justice and gives examples of "just" behavior and its importance in life.
      ISBN 0-8239-1231-0
      1. Justice—Juvenile literature. [1. Justice. 2. Conduct of life.] I. Title. II Series.
JC578.082   1992
320'.01'1—dc20   91-40100
                                                                                          CIP
                                                                                          AC

C O N T E N T S

INTRODUCTION

WHAT IS JUSTICE?

"I DON'T LIKE TO FAIL ANY STUDENT, JODIE," said Mr. Tyrone. "But in this case I have no choice. I saw you and Sara cheating on the test."

Jodie had always been one of Mr. Tyrone's very best students. She usually got A's and B's on her math tests. But Mr. Tyrone had seen Jodie hold her paper up in front of her. And he had seen Sara copying answers over Jodie's shoulder. To be fair to all the students who had *not* cheated, Mr. Tyrone had to punish any student who cheated. That was the only way to make sure everyone got the grades that he or she deserved.

Jodie, however, did not think Mr. Tyrone's decision was just. She saw the situation differently. After finishing the test, she checked her answers. She said that she had held up her paper to read through the test a second time. She had not known that Sara was copying from her paper.

6

Fortunately, Sara also felt that Jodie had been unfairly punished. After school, Sara went to Mr. Tyrone and told him the truth. "Jodie is innocent," Sara insisted. "She didn't know that I was copying answers from her test."

Mr. Tyrone was glad to hear the truth. He regraded Jodie's test and gave her a B+. And he decided to let Sara take a make-up test. Mr. Tyrone wanted to reward Sara's honesty by giving her a second chance.

Both Jodie and Mr. Tyrone wanted to see *justice* done. But they had a different point of view about what was just. Mr. Tyrone wanted to award grades fairly according to each student's performance. He believed that a student who didn't study and cheated should not get the same grade as a student who studied and didn't cheat. But Jodie felt Mr. Tyrone was punishing her for something she did not do.

Justice means that both rewards and punishments are handed out in a *just* manner. The word "just" has several meanings. It means trying your best to find out the truth or the facts. Once he discovered the truth about Sara's cheating, for example, Mr. Tyrone could reward and punish students more fairly.

Just treatment also means getting what you deserve. Jodie got the grade she earned. Sarah got a second chance for being honest. Both girls felt they had been treated justly.

> We expect justice and fairness in all aspects of our lives, from our families, our friends, teachers, and counselors.

Finally, being just means being fair. Fairness means being both *impartial* and *reasonable*. Impartial means *not* favoring one person over another. Mr. Tyrone treated both students alike. Reasonable means not going too far in either direction in punishments and rewards. Mr. Tyrone acted reasonably in giving Sara a second chance.

Justice means fairness in both punishment and rewards. One rule of justice demands that punishment fit the crime. Those who commit no crimes should not be punished. And for those who do commit crimes, punishment should be fair, reasonable, and impartial.

A second rule of justice is that rewards be earned according to what you deserve. For instance, a person who does better on a test should get a better grade. It would be unjust for a person's religion, sex, or skin color to affect the grade. This kind of treatment would not be fair.

Finally, justice means that everyone must have an equal chance to succeed. Just rewards are possible only if everyone has a fair chance to earn them.

Justice also means straightening out disputes fairly. When two people disagree, they should try to settle their disagreement justly. This means settling it based on the facts of the case. It means settling it so that each person gets what he or she deserves. And it means settling it fairly, impartially, and reasonably.

Different People See Justice Differently

Justice is important to everyone. Each of us wants to be treated fairly. We all want an equal chance to live in freedom, to succeed, and to be happy. When we do something right, we want to be justly rewarded. And when we do something wrong, we want our punishment to be fair.

But people often disagree about the best way to get justice. What one person thinks is fair another person might see as unfair. People also sometimes disagree about the "facts" involved in a particular case. Mr. Tyrone thought at first that both Jodie and Sara had cheated. Only when he heard more facts did he change his mind. This is why it is important to try to find out all of the facts. Justice depends on finding out the truth.

People can also disagree about what is a fair and just punishment. Some of Mr. Tyrone's students might have thought it just to fail Sara. After all, she did cheat on the test. But Mr. Tyrone thought justice would be better served by giving her a make-up test.

Different people see justice in different ways. People may agree on a definition of justice. But they may still disagree about how it works in a special case. What are the facts in a given situation? What settlement would be fair? These are day-to-day questions of justice.

A fair division of labor helps a family to function happily and makes each member feel that he or she is treated justly.

1

JUSTICE IN OUR LIVES

JUSTICE IS IMPORTANT TO US IN OUR DAY-TO-DAY LIVES on three different levels. The first is the way people deal with one another. The second level is how individuals are treated by the larger society. The third is how societies or nations relate to one another. Justice—or injustice—exists on all of these levels.

Person-to-Person

Individuals can treat one another justly or unjustly. Person-to-person justice plays a part in many different relationships. It can involve the relationship between student and teacher, as it did in Jodie's case. Justice is also present in the relationship between family members. Perhaps you and your sister both want to eat the last piece of apple pie. How could this argument be settled justly?

Many Americans were dedicated to the Persian Gulf War of 1990-1991 because they felt justice was served by liberating Kuwait from Iraqi invaders.

Justice can also come into play between a buyer and a seller. Suppose, for instance, that you buy a skateboard from a friend for $40. You would probably feel cheated if you then found out that two of the wheels were missing. How could you correct this injustice? You could demand your money back. Or perhaps your friend could keep the money, but fix the skateboard. Either of these actions would result in greater justice.

Justice is important in all of our relationships. But it also includes how we deal with friends, neighbors, and fellow students.

Sometimes the just treatment of other individuals will depend on your actions. Suppose that your school principal is punishing two students for fighting. If you saw the fight and know who started it, should you tell the principal the truth?

To answer this kind of question, it sometimes helps to imagine yourself in someone else's place. Imagine how you would feel if you were the student who had not started the fight. You would want the principal to treat you justly. So if someone knew what had really happened, you would want him or her to tell the truth. Unless the principal finds out the truth, he or she cannot provide justice.

Treating others the way we want to be treated is one way to promote justice. All of us want others to treat us

fairly. So we should treat others the same way. We need to try to be truthful and fair in our dealings with other people. In this way, we can help people in being just to one another.

Society-to-Individual

Justice is also important in the treatment of individuals by the larger *society*. A society is a group of people that have similar interests and beliefs. A church, a social club, and a nation are all examples of societies.

Sometimes societies treat certain individuals unjustly. Some societies punish or torture people for their beliefs or their race. During the 1930s and 1940s Nazi Germany unjustly arrested Jews, gypsies, and homosexuals. These victims of injustice had committed no crimes. They were arrested simply because the Nazis hated them. Millions of innocent men, women, and children were put in prison. They were tortured, and even murdered. This example of injustice shocked the world.

Some societies treat people unjustly because of their sex. Women in England and Canada could not vote in

---

elections until 1918. And the United States denied women the vote until 1920. In all three nations, women's receiving the right to vote helped change this injustice.

Other societies treat individuals unjustly because of their skin color. In South Africa, blacks have been denied the right to vote in elections. South African society also forbids blacks to live or work where they want. This great injustice has caused outrage and protest among South Africans and people throughout the world.

Society-to-Society

Just as individuals can treat one another either justly or unjustly, so can nations or societies. One example shows injustice in the dealings of nations. In August, 1990, Iraq invaded its small neighboring country of Kuwait. Kuwait had become an independent nation in 1961—but had been settled for almost 250 years. Iraq, however, claimed that it had owned all of Kuwait since ancient times. Within days, Iraq took control of Kuwait's oil fields. They seized the capital city, and drove the government out of the country.

Most of the other nations of the world regarded the Iraqi invasion of Kuwait as a serious injustice. The other nations quickly united to punish this injustice by cutting off all trade with Iraq. Countries refused to buy products made in Iraq and would not sell products to Iraq.

One of the foundations of justice is treating others the way you would like to be treated.

Some nations called for even more severe punishment. Nations began to discuss how to punish Iraq. Should other nations send soldiers to force Iraqi troops out of Kuwait? Some argued that this was the only quick way to restore justice. Others argued that the war itself would be an injustice. Thousands of people—Iraqis, Kuwaitis, and others—would die in such a war. Eventually, on January 17, 1991, that war began.

Throughout history, there have been many costly wars because of one society's unjust treatment of another. Nazi Germany, for example, invaded Austria, Czechoslovakia, and Poland in 1938 and 1939. Great Britain and France declared war on Germany within days of the Polish invasion. This war, World War II, soon involved people from almost every part of the world. By 1945, when the war ended, over 35 million people had died.

Most nations of the world no longer allow individuals to settle disputes through violence. Might does not make right between individuals.

Among nations, however, military might is still used to settle many disputes. Power, rather than truth or justice, decides many international disagreements. The nation that wins a war is not necessarily right. To bring about peace and justice, nations need to work harder to find peaceful means of settling disputes.

2

THE CHANGING FACE OF JUSTICE

THE DEBATE OVER FINDING A JUST REMEDY IN KUWAIT shows an important point about justice. Nearly everyone agrees on the need to defend and protect justice. But not everyone agrees on what justice is. Different generations, different societies, and different individuals see justice in different ways. Justice is not seen the same way by everyone.

The Beginnings of Justice

Early in history, people formed groups that today we call societies. Banding together in groups helped people protect themselves. The protection of the group needed everyone's cooperation. To survive, the society had to deal with any action that threatened to destroy this cooperation. These actions included not only crimes such as theft or murder, but also disagreements between people. If a person, for example, insulted someone or claimed that another person owed him or her money, the dispute had to be settled fairly.

In ancient societies, punishment of crime was the first and most important aspect of justice. These societies had to fight off wild animals and warring neighbors and struggle against harsh climates. Survival was at stake. The needs of the entire group had to come before the needs of the individual. To provide justice, therefore, meant punishing crimes against the group.

In time, the question of survival against harsh natural elements became less threatening. Communities grew larger and became more secure. The actions of any one individual seldom threatened the survival of the group. Group needs were then no longer the only concern of the community. Societies could pay more attention to the positive sides of justice. This meant rewarding good behavior to be sure that individuals got what they deserved. And it meant trying to give all individuals what they needed fairly.

Different Societies Have Different Views of Justice

Different societies see justice differently. Justice among the Eskimos is a good example. Until recently, the Eskimos

Ideas of justice differ from one culture to another. The Eskimos, for example, do not often deal with problems of theft because there is very little private property in traditional Eskimo culture.

had no private property. People shared everything to survive. So the Eskimos did not think stealing was a crime. Murdering or injuring someone who could hunt and fish, however, could harm the whole community. So the Eskimos did punish crimes of violence.

There were three punishments for murder. The lightest punishment made the criminal take care of the victim's family. The second punishment was death. The third was *banishment* forever from the tribe. This meant that the criminal could no longer stay in the community and would have to get along on his or her own. In the harsh climate of the Arctic, being alone meant slow death. This punishment was probably the worst of all.

Death or banishment of the murderer removed another hunter or fisher from the community. These punishments then threatened the group's survival as well. Yet the Eskimos saw violence as a very serious crime. Death or banishment not only punished the criminal, but it also made others afraid to commit murder.

Not all societies see death as a fair punishment—even for murder. Many countries—such as Brazil, Portugal, and Switzerland—do not punish *any* crimes with death. The people of these countries do not believe that the fear of death prevents anyone from committing murder. In addition, they see the death penalty as unreasonable punishment. They see the death penalty itself as unjust. So different societies define and apply justice in many different ways.

How Views of Justice Change over Time

Different generations also view justice in different ways. As societies grow stronger and more secure, for example, their ideas of justice change. When the survival of the society is in question, most societies begin to think of justice only in a negative way. The ideas of crime and punishment define justice in a negative way. Crimes tell what individuals do *not* have the right to do. Looking at justice this way tells what people *cannot* do.

When survival is not as important, the way we look at justice usually changes. The punishment of these crimes is still important. But protecting the group is no longer seen as the only aim of justice.

More secure societies also look at justice in more positive terms. Justice now concerns itself with protecting the *rights* of people too. Rights means the powers and privileges that all people have simply because they are people. The U.S. Declaration of Independence, for example, states that everyone has the right to "life, liberty, and the pursuit of happiness."

Chapter Two

The United Nations in New York City was created in 1945 to help bring justice to nations all over the world.

As societies grow, their ideas of justice begin to be both positive and negative. Justice not only describes and punishes crimes, it must also define and defend freedoms. In this way, the changing way we see justice tries to balance the rights of the group and the rights of individuals.

Time not only changes our ideas of what is just between society and the individual. Time also changes the way we look at justice between different societies.

The founding of the United Nations (U.N.) shows how our view of justice has changed. For centuries, war was the main way to settle arguments between nations. Victory in the war, however, did not always mean that justice had been done. It did not decide what was fair or right. Military strength, rather than justice, always won out.

By 1945, however, war was no longer seen as the best way to settle problems between nations. World War II had just ended with millions of deaths. And war had become much more dangerous. There were nuclear weapons that could destroy the entire planet.

In 1945, the U.N. was founded to try to settle disputes more peacefully and fairly. One goal of the U.N. was to establish justice among nations without going to war. Almost 50 years later, wars are still means of settling disputes. But nations can also turn to an organization dedicated to trying to settle disputes without going to war.

Punishment for crimes is one way our society enforces its laws and views of justice.

3

JUSTICE AND THE LAW

TO SUPPORT AND ENFORCE ITS VIEW OF JUSTICE, every society creates rules that people are expected to obey. These rules, which we call *laws,* show each society's ideas about justice. For this reason, laws of the nations are different but they also change throughout their history.

Laws on crime and punishment in ancient societies were most important. Even today, laws about crime and punishment are usually the first laws of a new society. Societies must try to make sure that crime doesn't pay. Otherwise, everyone might be tempted to commit crimes. The laws in most societies try to link punishments to fit the crimes against people or property.

Punishing criminals helps repair the injustice of the crime. In addition, punishment may set an example that keeps others from committing the same kind of crime. It reminds them to observe the rules of law. In this way,

just punishment protects the safety of all citizens in that society fairly.

The protection of group safety is the most important reason to have laws. Even the most basic laws advance justice. Punishing wrong actions, for example, tries to keep criminals from profiting from their crimes. But the best laws bring about both order and justice.

A Society's Laws Show How People View Justice

Laws almost always show a society's beliefs. As a society's ideas change, the laws of that society usually change too. Laws change to reflect differences in the way the society sees the doing of justice itself. Laws can also change to show the way society thinks about such issues as individual rights, reasonable punishment, and impartiality.

Individual Rights. The earliest laws of a society protect society as a whole. Laws define crimes and set punishments. Laws also establish a *judicial system* for the society. The government of a society enforces laws. Its judicial system decides whether laws are applied fairly.

More secure societies, however, tend to see justice in the things citizens should do as well as what they should not do. New laws have to give these balanced definitions

Our judicial system asks
the judges and juries to
decide on the guilt of an
accused person through
the process of a fair trial.

---

of justice. These new laws clearly spell out and defend
individual rights and freedoms. In this way, laws protect
people from power used unfairly against them, especially
by the government. Such laws see to it that the individual
is treated fairly by society.

Many nations today have passed laws making sure that
people's rights are protected. Canada, for example, protects
individual rights through its Charter of Rights and Freedoms.
The United States protects these same rights through the
Bill of Rights. The Bill of Rights is made up of the first
ten amendments to the U.S. Constitution. The First
Amendment, for instance, guarantees freedom of religion,
speech, writing, the press, and the right to assemble
peaceably.

Such laws say that using these freedoms cannot be
called crimes. People cannot be punished for believing or
saying or writing what they believe. The right to meet
peaceably lets people protest against unfairness without
fear of punishment. These laws try to protect people
from unfair government power.

As history has continued, the idea of justice has
permitted more and more basic rights and freedoms. Today
most societies believe, for instance, that every person
should have the right to a fair trial. Everyone should have
the right to go to school. Everyone should have the right
to earn a decent living. People should have the right to

Unjust laws still exist today. In South Africa, many people have fought to end the government's practice of apartheid. Protesters are saying that segregation does not provide equal justice for people of all races.

worship—or not worship—their god. And people should have a right to take part in their government.

As the permitting of rights grows, new laws show the change in the views about justice today. The laws of many societies today guarantee the protection of these individual rights.

Reasonable Punishment. Throughout history, society's changing ideas of justice have brought about changes in the law concerning suitable punishments. The ideas about which punishment fits a crime change from one society to another. They also change over time. The kinds of punishments allowed by a society show how that society understands justice.

The laws of many societies are like views of justice found in the Bible. The Book of Exodus has broad rules of punishment for crimes:

"Thou shalt give life for life,/Eye for eye, tooth for tooth, hand for hand, foot for foot,/Burning for burning, wound for wound, stripe for stripe." (Exodus 21:23-25)

This rule could be taken simply to mean let the punishment fit the crime. Some cultures, however, have exactly followed these rules of justice. Thieves have had their hands cut off. Those who cursed or spoke against God or the government had their tongues cut out. This kind of "eye for eye" justice is still widespread.

When the rules are broken
in organized sports, justice
demands a fit punishment.

Today, an "eye for an eye" is no longer considered fit punishment. It is fit only for revenge. But revenge is *not* concerned with justice. It seeks to inflict equal—or often worse—damage on a criminal. Revenge does not respond to injustice with reason and fairness.

Many societies have enacted laws that outlaw the kinds of extreme punishments that border on revenge. England, Canada, and the United States, for example, all forbid the use of "cruel and unusual punishments." Cutting off body parts, public whippings, and the burning of people suspected of being witches are no longer considered fit punishments for crimes. Such severe punishments would themselves be injust.

The death penalty is one punishment that has changed to show a new understanding of justice. In ancient times, the Bible described death as an appropriate punishment for murder. But it was also considered appropriate for hitting or cursing a parent, witchcraft, and bestiality.

Today, the death sentence is regarded as an unjustly harsh punishment for minor crimes. Indeed, some people wonder whether the death penalty ever delivers justice, even in murder cases. Many people wonder whether the death penalty serves the interests of justice or simply the desire for revenge. For this reason, many nations have outlawed the death penalty altogether.

Impartiality. In paintings and sculpture, justice is usually pictured as a blindfolded woman balancing scales. Most cultures aim toward the ideal of the "blindness of justice." But what exactly does this mean? It reflects the belief that justice should be impartial. It should be blind to everything but the facts.

Justice should decide questions of right and wrong, guilt and innocence, on the basis of facts alone. Justice should be blind in delivering both individual rights and punishments. Justice should protect and punish every individual equally. Justice should not "see" sex, skin color, religion, or wealth. Justice should be "blind" to considerations of power, fame, or influence. This is our ideal vision of what justice should be.

The United States Supreme Court is the highest court in the country. The Court's nine justices must make decisions that affect laws across the nation.

But in practice, justice is not so blind. Wealth, for example, has a great influence on the process of justice. Crimes committed by the poor can often be punished more harshly than those committed by the rich. The wealthy can often hire more skillful lawyers to defend them. In addition, judges and juries tend to regard wealthy criminals as less of a threat than poor criminals. Justice is also not truly blind to an individual's religion, race, sex, or color.

Justice has become more blind, however, through the efforts of individuals like Thurgood Marshall. Marshall, a lawyer and Supreme Court Justice, fought to make justice blind to skin color. From 1938 to 1961 he won 29 of the 32 cases he argued before the Supreme Court. Marshall argued that the law must protect the rights of African Americans and whites equally. As a result of his cases, African Americans won the same rights as whites to vote in primary elections, to sit wherever they want on inter-state buses, and to enter law school.

In 1954, Marshall argued his most famous case: *Brown v. Board of Education.* After the court's ruling, schools could no longer separate pupils according to race. It was unjust to let schools deny equal education only because of skin color.

No society may ever reach the ideal of blind justice. Yet all societies need to keep working toward this ideal.

Justice demands even-handed and fair treatment of every individual. And to reach this goal, justice cannot be blinded by wealth, power, or color.

Laws Are Not Always Just

Justice and the law are not the same. Ideally, the law supports justice. But governments set up laws first to maintain order and second to promote justice.

Slavery, for example, was part of the way society was organized in the United States until 1865. In that year, following the end of the Civil War, the Thirteenth Amendment to the Constitution ruled that slavery was against the law. Laws before the Civil War preserved slavery in society. In doing so, the laws of many states allowed white citizens to own slaves. In this way, America promoted injustice rather than justice.

Unjust laws still exist today. In South Africa, the *apartheid* (pronounced "apart-hate") laws treat people differently depending upon their race. Whites hold almost all political and economic power in the country. Blacks are denied many rights. The law forbids blacks to take part in government. They cannot hold certain jobs. And they cannot live where they want. Laws like these uphold an unjust and racist system.

There must be laws to protect the common good of any society. But laws must balance the rights of both society

Laws and justice are not always the same thing. In America, slavery was legal for hundreds of years. It was not until after the Civil War in 1865 that laws about slavery were changed.

and the individual. Laws that protect society but greatly damage individual rights are unjust. Laws must also remain fair and impartial. Laws that benefit one group over another are unjust.

Since not all laws are just, each of us needs to examine our laws with a critical eye. And whenever we discover unjust laws, we have the responsibility to speak out against them.

America's Founders created our Constitution in 1787. Today the Constitution still serves as the foundation for all our laws, rights, and freedoms.

4

JUSTICE THROUGH GOVERNMENT

MOST NATIONS TRY TO ACHIEVE JUSTICE through their government. Government uses two different ways to attain justice. First, it makes general laws that define crimes, protect rights, and set punishments. Second, it applies these general laws to specific cases.

Lawmaking

Many nations, including Canada and the United States, enact new laws according to a written *constitution*. A constitution states the powers of a government. It is thought of as the highest law of the land. All new laws must follow the laws of a nation's constitution. The constitution guides the citizens who make and write the nation's laws.

Many modern constitutions include a bill of rights. This document protects its people from the possible injustice of their government. The English Bill of Rights, passed by Parliament in 1689, limited the power of the king. It also granted certain rights to those accused of crimes, and it guaranteed fundamental individual freedoms such as speech and writing. Both the United States and Canada based their bills of rights on the English Bill of Rights. Bills of rights have greatly advanced the cause of justice in countries that have them.

A nation's constitution and bill of rights are guides in the creation of new laws. Since our views of justice change with time, our laws must also change. For this reason, every society has to have a method of changing laws. Lawmakers must have the means to change general laws so they agree with current ideas and beliefs.

A look back in American history shows how changing views of justice led to new laws. In the early 1800s, many white Americans wrongly viewed African Americans as "less than human." This view was used to defend slavery. African Americans were treated as property, rather than as people.

Throughout the century, however, many white views of African Americans changed. More whites slowly began to realize that African Americans deserved equal human rights. And the nation enacted laws that showed this changed view. The Thirteenth Amendment, passed in

1865, outlawed slavery throughout the United States. This important law corrected one of the greatest injustices of our nation's history.

Three years later, the Fourteenth Amendment brought more justice to African Americans. It required states to provide "equal protection of the laws" to all of its citizens. The laws of many states had treated whites and African Americans differently. The injustice of this policy was declared illegal by the Fourteenth Amendment. This amendment promised justice to all regardless of race, religion, color, or sex.

Since the middle of the nineteenth century, many new laws have further recognized the basic rights of African Americans. The courts have enforced and extended these laws. Among the cases that Thurgood Marshall argued before the Supreme Court before he himself became a justice were measures that extended "equal protection" to questions of voting rights and education. During the 1960s, protests and movements were organized by African Americans. These demonstrations brought other injustices into full view. The law now guarantees African Americans and white Americans the same rights to vote, to pursue their education, and to live and work where they want. This is a good example of how laws change as society changes its view of what is just.

The Magna Carta, signed by England's King John in 1215, outlined the rights of people to receive "fair" and impartial justice.

Judicial Systems

All nations establish judicial systems, or systems of justice, in an attempt to give justice equally to all members of a society. Judicial systems carry out the laws of the land. They apply general laws to specific cases.

The judicial systems of both Canada and the United States have strong links to the British system of justice. In Great Britain's early history, the king handed out all justice. The country's nobles, however, felt the king did not deliver justice impartially. To avoid being overthrown, King John signed the *Magna Carta* (Latin for "great charter") in 1215. The Magna Carta was the first English document that outlined what people then thought was the "proper" course of justice.

The Magna Carta promised justice to all members of the nobility. It guaranteed accused noblemen the right to a trial by a jury of their peers. It established trial courts to help deliver justice. Centuries later, England granted these rights to all of its citizens, rather than just its nobles. Both the United States and Canada adopted much of the British judicial system. The workings of trial courts in particular owe a great deal to the British system of justice.

The courts. Most judicial systems employ courts, judges, and juries to deliver justice. The courts in most western countries are formed to do three things. 1) They carry out and enforce the law through holding trials and sentencing. 2) They attempt to settle disputes fairly and without violence. 3) They examine laws to make sure they remain just. All three of these may also involve punishing and/or correcting unjust or abusive treatment.

In the United States and Canada, both the federal government and individual states or provinces operate a number of trial courts. These are the courts in which most trials occur. Federal and local (state or provincial) courts try both criminal and civil cases.

Criminal courts. These courts decide cases in which
the state has accused someone of breaking a law. This
includes cases of violent crime such as assault, rape, and
murder. Criminal courts also try cases of less or nonviolent crimes such as theft, fraud, vandalism, drug
trafficking, spying, and treason.

Civil courts. These courts settle disputes between two
parties. The law refers to the participants in a civil lawsuit
as parties. Parties in a lawsuit may be people, businesses,
organizations, or the government. One party, the *plaintiff,*
sues another party, the *defendant,* for causing damages to
its person or property. An unshoveled walkway may
have caused a neighbor to fall and break a hip. Or
perhaps a newspaper printed lies that damaged someone's
good name. The party injured by any of these actions can
sue to obtain justice. The civil court aims to restore
justice peacefully to someone injured by the actions of
another.

Sometimes a civil suit involves a criminal action. For
instance, someone hit by a drunken driver can sue the
driver. The plaintiff may demand money to pay for
medical bills or time lost from work, but the state may still
bring criminal charges against the defendant. The criminal
and civil trials will be held separately.

In a criminal or civil trial, lawyers for each side present
witnesses, evidence, and arguments in an attempt to

prove their case. They may simply try to disprove the other side's case. A judge oversees the trial and makes sure that the trial remains fair to both sides. A judge or jury listens to both sides of the disagreement and then decides if any wrong has been done. If the defendant in a criminal trial is found guilty, the judge then decides fair punishment. In a civil suit, if the plaintiff wins, a judgment about the cost of the damages caused by the defendant is also needed.

Unfortunately, trial courts do not always deliver justice. For this reason, appeals courts serve as watchdogs over the lower courts. An appeals court reviews trial court rulings to make sure they are fair. In this way, they can correct possible injustices committed in the trial courts. Defendants can ask for an appeal if they believe the trial ruling, the sentence, or the award of damages in a civil suit was unfair.

The appeals court judges may agree with the lower court's decision if they believe it has been just. But if they decide there is a serious injustice, the appeals court may reverse the lower court's decision. Or it may order a new trial in the lower court. Defendants or plaintiffs can appeal the decisions of appeals courts to even higher courts.

In both Canada and the United States, the Supreme Court has the final word on whether justice has been done. The Supreme Court goes over lower court records

Chapter Four

All of us, no matter what we are accused of, have the right to due process. That means everyone has the right to a fair trial and is considered innocent until proven guitly.

and studies its rulings. The Supreme Court also examines the laws that apply in each case it reviews. The Supreme Court makes sure the laws remain just and agree with the nation's constitution. (The Supreme Court—and lower courts—can strike down laws that violate a nation's constitution.) The Supreme Court gives the final ruling on the cases it has accepted. Defendants or plaintiffs cannot appeal their case any further.

Due process. The guarantee of due process is the most important principle of justice on which all judicial systems rest. Due process describes the rules that govern a nation's justice system. The government of many nations cannot take a person's life, liberty, or property without due process of law. The rules of due process protect the legal rights of those accused or even suspected of committing a crime. They try to be sure that everyone gets a fair trial.

The Magna Carta set down the rights of the accused for the first time in the English language. The Charter of Rights and Freedoms describes due process in Canada. In the United States, the rules of due process are described in the Bill of Rights, especially the Fourth through Eighth Amendments.

Many elements of due process apply to the justice systems in a wide variety of countries, including Great Britain, Canada, and the United States. One of the most important parts of due process guarantees the accused the right to a jury trial. This right applies to serious criminal cases and also to many civil cases. The trial should take place as quickly as possible, because a defendant may be innocent. In addition, the trial should be held in public, to help insure fairness.

A key element of due process in the United States and Canada is the "presumption of innocence." A judge and jury must always assume the defendant in a criminal trial is innocent until proven guilty. Being charged with a crime does not mean being guilty of that crime. Lawyers must prove the crime. They must prove the guilt of the defendant "beyond a reasonable doubt." The defendant does not have to prove his or her innocence.

Both Canada and the United States forbid unreasonable searches or seizures of individuals or any of their property. Searching or arresting a person without good reason violates the idea of innocence. A judge must first grant permission, known as a *warrant*, before law officers can arrest a person. Officers must have a search warrant to search someone or search an individual's property. Evidence gained illegally (without a warrant) cannot be used against a defendant in court.

Due process guarantees accused persons a fair chance to defend themselves. Defendants must be told what crimes they are accused of committing. This permits them to prepare a proper defense. And defendants also have the right to seek help from a lawyer in preparing their defense. Defendants have the right to face their accusers and attempt to disprove their charges. In addition, defendants have the right to *force* witnesses to speak the truth in their defense.

Canada and the United States allow defendants to refuse to provide evidence that might be used against them. All defendants have the right to remain silent. Police cannot use torture or violence in an attempt to force a suspect to confess to a crime. Even if a defendant refuses to speak, however, a jury must assume his or her innocence unless proven guilty.

Every citizen has an equal right to the due process of law. The elements of due process thus provide the best guarantee that the law treats everyone equally and fairly.

How well do judicial systems work? They certainly work better than deciding disputes with fighting or violence. They offer most of us some protection from the abuse of power. Judicial systems do provide some measure of justice. Still, no system works perfectly all of the time. Laws are not necessarily all good and just. Judicial systems have flaws and make mistakes. The courts cannot guarantee justice in every case.

Sometimes a court commits an injustice, punishing a person for crimes he or she did not commit. A famous case of this kind of injustice occurred in Scottsboro, Alabama, in the 1930s. Nine African American youths were charged with raping two white women. During the trial, doctors testified that no rape had occurred. But the jury ignored this testimony. The "Scottsboro Boys" did not receive a fair trial because they had dark skin. The jury found them guilty of rape. Eight of the youths were sentenced to death. These unjust convictions were later reversed. But some of the youths had already spent six years or more in jail.

No justice system provides perfect justice in every case. For this reason, individual citizens cannot rely simply on laws and the courts to insure justice. We too need to act as watchdogs who guard against injustice. We need to examine the actions of individuals, businesses, the government, and the courts. And we need to question the laws themselves. Whenever we see an injustice, we must demand justice. Justice depends upon all of us.

5

JUSTICE THROUGH THE PEOPLE

JUSTICE IS CERTAINLY HARD TO WIN. Yet we still need to aim toward the ideal of "justice for all." Each of us needs to do what we can to bring about equal justice. And often this means taking action to defend justice or fight injustice. When government cannot bring about justice, the people must attempt to achieve it in some other way.

Revolts and Uprisings

People need to see that the law is just. It must protect their own safety, security, and rights as well as it protects those of others. Laws that fail to provide equal protection to all of a nation's citizens are themselves unjust. And many people refuse to obey laws that they consider to be unjust.

The refusal to obey laws often becomes a *revolt*. Soweto, South Africa, was the site of one such revolt. Soweto's residents—blacks whom whites had forced out

of the city of Johannesburg—demanded equality for many
years. In 1976, the government passed a law that made
all African schools teach in the Afrikaans language, the
language of the whites in power. Many blacks opposed
this law. They saw it as another attempt by the nation's
powerful whites to dominate the country's blacks.

Students soon organized a march to protest against the
injustice of this law. The South African government used
the police and army to crush the developing revolt. The
Soweto Uprising, three weeks of fierce fighting, resulted.
The police and army destroyed homes, arrested thousands
of protesters, and killed almost 600 people. The government crushed the revolt. But their brutality helped gain
worldwide support for equal justice in South Africa.

Even revolts that fail can help advance the cause of
justice. The famous Soweto Uprising did not lead to any
immediate correction of injustice. Yet it brought the
injustice of apartheid to the world's attention. And this
increased the pressure on the South African government
to provide justice to *all* of its citizens.

Individuals Who Have Fought for Justice

Individuals who have the courage to stand up for what
they believe can also bring about justice. The champions
of justice demand changes to correct injustice. And they

The Soweto Uprising of
1976 was a tragic example
of the high price many
people must pay for
justice.

Nelson Mandela has spent
his life fighting for equal
justice in South Africa.

---

also do whatever they can to correct injustice. Two such champions of justice are Jane Addams and Nelson Mandela.

Jane Addams, Social Reformer

Jane Addams took up the cause of justice on many fronts. In the 1880s, Addams became concerned about the unjust treatment of poor people. The poor were denied proper housing and good education. Addams felt it was unjust for the poor to have so little when the rich had so much. She became convinced that living among the poor was the only way to insure them justice.

In 1889, Addams opened Hull House in a very poor neighborhood in Chicago. Lawyers, artists, educators, and social workers who lived at Hull House took part in hands-on *social reform.* (Social reformers aim to change society in order to make it more just.) They supplied daycare, gymnasiums, education, and schooling in art and music to the poor community.

Addams soon realized that providing services was not enough to deliver justice to the poor. Working conditions for poor people were unjust and even inhuman. Addams fought for labor laws that would eliminate the abuse of workers by factories and other employers. She also demanded child labor laws to protect children from the mistreatment of employers.

Addams also felt that the courts treated children unjustly. She did not think it fair to treat children who committed crimes as if they were adults. Her crusade against this injustice led to the foundation of the nation's first juvenile court in 1899. Addams was awarded the 1931 Nobel Peace Prize in recognition of her many efforts to advance the cause of justice.

Nelson Mandela, South Africa's Civil Rights Leader

Nelson Mandela has committed his life to the struggle for justice in South Africa. Mandela helped lead the fight to win human and political rights for South African blacks.

As a 25-year-old lawyer Mandela joined the African National Congress (ANC) in 1944. The ANC tried to correct injustice through nonviolent direct action. Mandela and the ANC used labor strikes and work stoppages as weapons against South African apartheid. In the 1950s, Mandela headed the ANC's Defiance Against Unjust Laws Campaign. He and thousands of others broke apartheid laws at the risk of lengthy prison terms.

The Sharpeville massacre in March 1960 changed Mandela's approach to ending apartheid. Police had killed 69 unarmed black protesters and wounded 86 others. The South African government had met peaceful demands with violence.

The Guardian Angels is a private group that tries to defend citizens against crime by patrolling city streets.

Mandela became convinced that nonviolent protest would no longer work. He headed a branch of the ANC that committed *sabotage*. This meant that they destroyed buildings or other targets that symbolized apartheid. Mandela, however, refused to commit violent acts against any people.

In 1964, a non-jury trial found Nelson Mandela guilty of sabotage and treason. He was sentenced to life in prison. Discussion or printing of Mandela's political views was banned. Mandela was considered a "non-person"—someone who no longer existed in the eyes of the law.

In prison, Mandela became a symbol of the struggle of black South Africans for justice. Campaigns to "Free Mandela" sprang up in countries all over the world. On February 11, 1990, Mandela was released from prison.

Twenty-seven years in prison had not bowed his pride or his commitment to justice. Mandela immediately demanded that the South African government release all other political prisoners. He repeated his support of all ANC policies. He called for talks to develop a new constitution for South Africa. And he insisted that the government grant all political and human rights to blacks.

In May, 1990, Mandela and the ANC formally met with the South African government. Both groups agreed that some progress had been made. Yet Mandela's struggle for justice in South Africa continues to this day.

Organizations that Fight for Justice

Organizations can also fight for justice and against injustice. The United Nations, for example, attempts to promote peaceful and fair interaction among the countries of the world. The U.N. operates the International Court of Justice, also known as the World Court. This court is intended to settle serious disputes among nations fairly, reasonably, and impartially. In this way, nations have a means of securing justice without going to war. Membership in the U.N. has tripled since 1945. Today, over 160 countries belong to the United Nations.

Amnesty International (AI). This organization, founded in London in 1961, fights against government abuse of individual rights. AI publicizes violations of human rights and freedoms in countries all over the world. The organization is especially concerned about governments that unjustly imprison people, torture them, and sometimes kill them. Members of AI write letters of protest to governments that commit these injustices. The organization demands the release of people imprisoned for attempting to exercise their freedom of speech, press, assembly, or religion. Today, Amnesty International, which won the 1977 Nobel Peace Prize, has over 200,000 members in 100 countries.

The champions of justice are everywhere. As this chapter shows, anyone, anywhere can defend justice and fight injustice. It doesn't matter where you live or what occupation you choose. Champions of justice include former slaves, wealthy young women, journalists, artists, mothers, ex-convicts, and lawyers. So whoever you are, whatever you do, you too can stand up for justice.

6

RECOGNIZING AND BATTLING INJUSTICE

THE HISTORY OF HUMANKIND IS A CONTINUING STRUGGLE toward the ideal of justice for all. No matter how many victories we gain, however, this struggle will never be over. The cause of justice requires all of us to remain on our guard. We need to be alert to the injustice around us. And we need to fight against the injustices we see.

Dr. Martin Luther King, Jr., eloquently expressed this idea in a famous letter written in 1963. King led African Americans in their struggle for justice in the 1950s and 1960s. One such protest in Birmingham, Alabama, turned ugly. Police beat protesters, aimed powerful fire hoses at them, and turned attack dogs on them. Yet thousands risked injury, arrest, and death to protest for equal human and political rights.

King and hundreds of others were jailed for their part in the protest. Yet King vowed to continue the struggle

despite the violence of the unjust. King pledged his commitment to justice in his famous "Letter from Birmingham Jail." He smuggled the letter out of jail on scraps of paper, newsprint, and toilet paper. "Injustice anywhere is a threat to justice everywhere," he wrote.

We cannot knowingly allow any one person to suffer from injustice. Justice for all cannot exist if fair treatment is denied to any individual. The best way to protect justice for ourselves is to promote just treatment toward all others. This means not only that we need to treat others fairly. We also need to make sure that *everyone* treats others fairly.

As King noted, we cannot turn our backs on injustice anywhere in the world. We need to recognize that every person in the world is connected to every other. These

Recognizing and Battling Injustice

During the 1960s, young African Americans sat at an "all-white" lunch counter in the South as a way to protest U.S. laws about segregation.

---

connections mean that a single injustice can endanger or destroy justice for all. For this reason, we need to fight any injustice anywhere in the world.

The fight for justice often begins on the neighborhood level. Jane Addams opened a settlement house to bring justice to the poor of her neighborhood. Yet her example inspired countless others to copy her.

Look around your own neighborhood. Do you notice any injustice going on there? Perhaps your school principal denies the right to free speech by censoring the school newspaper. Maybe a local club refuses to admit certain members because of the color of their skin. You may see the police arrest the wrong person for a crime. Or perhaps a fellow student is taking credit for something you know he didn't do. Maybe you notice a store owner cheating his or her customers. Your local government may ignore the problems of the poor and homeless. Whenever you notice injustices like these, fight against them. Stand up for what you know is right.

Defending justice against common beliefs is not easy. In the struggle for justice we may need to risk verbal abuse, arrest, and even violence. Yet the ideal of justice for all cannot be compromised. Each of us needs to do what we know is just. And we need to defend what we know is just. Only through such courage can we move toward our common goal of justice for all.

Glossary: *Explaining New Words*

apartheid A political and economic system in South Africa. It allows the government's unjust and unequal treatment of non-whites.

banishment Punishing a criminal by forcing him or her to leave society.

constitution A document that defines the powers of a government; the supreme law of the land.

crime Any action that society says a person has no right to do.

defendant A person, group, or institution that is charged with a crime.

due process of law The rules that govern a nation's system of justice; the elements of a fair trial.

impartial Treating everyone equally.

injustice An action that violates the rights of others; an unfair punishment or action against other people.

just True or deserved; fair and reasonable.

justice Fairness in both punishment and reward.

Magna Carta The first document in the English language to describe a proper course for justice. It also guaranteed certain rights for those accused of crime.

party One of the sides in a lawsuit.

plaintiff A person, group, or institution that charges another person, group, or institution with an injustice.

presumption of innocence The belief that a person accused of a crime is innocent until proven guilty.

revenge Seeking to punish an injustice (often with another injustice).

revolt A refusal to obey laws or rules.

rights Basic powers and privileges that belong to everyone in a society.

suffrage The right to vote.

warrant A judge's permission that allows the search of a suspect's property or the arrest of a suspect.

For Further Reading

Benson, Mary. *Nelson Mandela*. London: Hamish
   Hamilton, 1986. This biography portrays Mandela's
   life and his fight for justice in South Africa. It offers
   a glimpse of his struggle against apartheid until his
   imprisonment in 1963.

David, Andrew. *Famous Supreme Court Cases*.
   Minneapolis: Lerner Publications Company, 1980.
   This book describes some of the most important
   cases ever decided by the Supreme Court.

Feuerlicht, Roberta Strauss. *In Search of Peace*. New
   York: Julian Messner, 1970. The author relates the
   stories of four Americans who won the Nobel
   Peace Prize. It includes portraits of social reformers
   Jane Addams and Martin Luther King, Jr.

O'Connor, Karen. *Homeless Children*. San Diego: Lucent
   Books, 1989. This book provides a very moving
   exploration of the problems of the homeless
   throughout the United States. It focuses particularly
   on the hardships of children and teenagers.

INDEX

About the Author

Kevin Osborn, a free-lance writer and editor, has written over two dozen books for children and adults, including *Tolerance* for *The Values Library* series. He has coauthored several volumes in the *American Heritage History of the United States* series. In addition, Mr. Osborn created the characters for the young adult fiction series *Not Quite Human,* which served as the basis for two Disney Productions television movies of the same name.

Photo Credits and Acknowledgments

Cover photo: ©Diana Walker/Gamma-Liaison
Photos on page 2, 10, 15, 30: Jill Heisler Jacks; page 9: Stuart Rabinowitz; pages 13, 32, 35, 36, 41, 44, 53, 58: Wide World Photos; page 19: ©L. Cottrell/Gamma-Liaison; page 22: Bruce Glassman; page 24: ©John Chiasson/Gamma-Liaison; page 27: ©Frank Fisher/Gamma-Liaison; pages 28, 29: ©Isabel Ellsen/Gamma-Liaison; page 51: Gamma-Liaison

Design and Production: Blackbirch Graphics, Inc.